THE RELIGIOUS POEMS OF
Emma Catherine Embury

CHARLES RUSSELL
EDITOR

Table of Contents

Introduction to Emma Embury's Religious Poems...1

Confidence in God...5

    To the Evening Star...5

    A Litany..7

    Peace...9

    Song...10

    Sunset...11

    Stanzas..12

    Sonnet...14

Holy Chronicles..15

    Christ in the Tempest..15

    The Hymn in the Tempest..17

    The Pool of Bethesda...21

    The Moravian Burial Ground...23

    Byron in Certosa Cemetery..26

Heartache..29

    A Lament...29

    The Mother's Solace..30

    Stanzas on the Death of a Sister...31

    Elegaic Stanzas..32

    The Mourner's Appeal...33

    Epitaphs on a Young Lady...34

    Stanzas..34

    Fragment...36

    Stanzas..38

    Stanzas..39

Inquietude..39

Fragment...40

Sonnet 41

Something Beyond 42

Courage...43

Sonnet 43

Sonnet 43

Sabbath Morning 44

Confidence in Heaven..45

Devotion 46

How Will Ye Think of Me 46

"Dum Spiro, Spero" 48

INTRODUCTION TO EMMA EMBURY'S RELIGIOUS POEMS

Call her majestic. The most popular woman poet of America's early 19th Century literary Renaissance. She was deeply religious. More than forty of her devotional poems appeared in newspapers and magazines during her writing career. Edgar Allen Poe, who published many of her secular essays, observed that she was always original. In that respect it's important to realize she was writing for the general public, so her religious poems traverse the full range of spiritual topics – Confidence in God, Holy Chronicles, Heartache, Courage.

Born February 1, 1806, the daughter of Elizabeth Post-Manley and Dr. James Manley, a scientist and leader of New York medicine, at twenty-two she married Daniel Embury, a successful banker who wrote poetry and admired and aided her literary career. They had five children, Anna, James, Catharine, Daniel, and Philip.

Her daughter Anna wrote a *Memoir* that portrays Emma's dedication to God. *It was always her habit to go to the nursery immediately after the evening meal, when she talked with us about the little faults and failings of the day, sometimes telling us stories, then preparing us for bed, and hearing us say our prayers.*

Regarding the *Moravian Burial Ground* poem, Daniel's ancestors came from the Palatinate region bordering the Rhine in western Germany. Emma's poem with that title takes place in a cemetery started by people from an eastern district of Germany that today is part of the Czech Republic. Both groups settled in Pennsylvania and were called the "Pennsylvania Dutch." Emma's use of the word "our" in the poem undoubtedly means that she and Daniel visited the burial ground together. Her introduction to the poem reads, *The following lines are an attempt to convey an idea of the simple beauty of the Moravian Burial Ground in Bethlehem, Pennsylvania. The feelings described suggested themselves on the spot, and the incident alluded to actually occurred.*

The Englishman Lord George Byron was one of Emma's favorite poets. He moved to Ravenna in Italy after he left England in disgrace over numerous scandalous love affairs. While there (1819-1822) he visited Certosa Cemetery in nearby Bologna. Struck by an epitaph on a tomb, he wrote a letter to Richard Belgrave Hoppner (the son of John Hoppner, who painted his lover the Countess of Oxford Jane Elizabeth Scott's portrait) saying, *I found such a pretty epitaph, or rather two: one was, 'Marsini Luigi, implora pace.' The other 'Lucrezia Picini, implora eterna quiete.' That was all, but it appeared to me that these two or three wordletts comprise and express all that can be said on the subject. They contain doubt, hope, humility. Let me have 'Implora pace,' and nothing else, for my epitaph.*

Emma quoted this passage as the lead to *Byron in Certosa Cemetery*. The poem tells how he was caught in a world of care and want; how he left pleasure's wine cup to free the Greek nation from the Ottoman Empire; how he became as famous for that quest as for his poetry; how he learned of earth's hopes, its pride, its woe, its joy, its pain; how he came to seek eternal rest, "Wishing," as Emma put it, "to drink from death's dark stream, his feverish spirit's thirst to slake."

A Lament, the first poem in the Heartache series, was written by Emma for her brother, Joseph Manley, who died in an accident at sea. Anna's *Memoir* tells of the event:

My mother was the second child of Dr. and Mrs. Manley. The first, a bright, handsome youth, became infatuated with the idea of being a sailor, and on his second voyage at some place unknown to me, on a bright, sunny day, in ight of land, the ship struck on a rock. Every soul on board perished except one man who escaped to tell the pitiful tale.

A Mother's Solace, the second prayer in the Heartache series, is an epitaph for Emma's daughter Catharine, who died in 1837. Anna reported the heartbreaking event in her *Memoir*:

Our sister, a wonderfully beautiful child, died when four and a half years old, of dropsy on the brain, caused by a fall out of bed. Just after this happened, she went to visit at grandfather Manley's, was taken ill there, and died the 29th of March, preceding the death of aunt Emma the following June.

Mother was so devoted to her children that it was a long time before she could rally or recover from the great loss and bereavement. It was always her habit to go to the nursery immediately after the evening meal, when she talked with us about the little faults and failings of the day, sometimes telling us stories, then preparing us for bed, and hearing us say our prayers. She told me that for several weeks after our sister's death, almost every evening she had a distinct vision of her, clad in her nightrobe, coming from the direction of the door, with outstretched arms towards her. It was so real that the impulse was to spring to meet her, but it was momentary, and the lovely vision would vanish.

In her middle age Emma wrote *Stanzas on the Death of a Sister* in mourning for her sister Petronella Manley, who died at the age of thirty-three on March 16, 1850. Sad to say, Emma may have exhausted her powers of writing mourning poetry, because she wrote none when her mother died on April 3 and her father on November 21 in 1851.

The climax of Emma's religious poems lies in the Courage series. The Sonnets are primary because they embody the reactions of devout persons to the rise of evolutionary theory. In the Sonnets Emma addresses the work of Robert Chalmers, whose *Vestiges of Natural History of Creation*, was published in1844 fifteen years before Darwin's *Origin of the Species*. The daughter of an eminent scientifically trained physician, Emma accepted Chalmers' work as one of "the truths of Science," but lamented what would happen if "Earth" —

> Her lifted eye of prayer could only see
> Necessity's stern laws graven on eternity.

And —

> Alas! for those who quench the holy spark
> Of inspiration in their secret soul

Which she followed with her defiance of life's ills and her triumphant, *Dum Spiro, Spero.*

CONFIDENCE IN GOD

TO THE EVENING STAR

Pale, melancholy star! that pourest thy beams
So mildly on my brow, pure as the tear
A pitying angel sheds o'er earthly sorrow,
I love to sit beneath thy light, and yield
My heart to its strange musings, wayward dreams
Of things inscrutable, and searching thoughts
That would aspire to dwell in yon high sphere.
I love to think that thou art a bright world
Where bliss and beauty dwell — where never sin
Has entered to destroy the perfect joys
Of its pure holy habitants. 'Tis sweet
To fancy such a quiet peaceful home
Of innocence, and purity, and love.

There the first sire still dwells with all his race,
From his loved eldest-born to the sweet babe
Of yesterday; there gentle maids are seen,
Fair as the sun, with all that tenderness
So sweet in woman; and soft eyes that beam
The fondest love, but freed from passion's stain.
There all have high communion with their God,
And though the fruit of knowledge is not plucked,
Yet doth its fragrance breathe on all around.
O! what can knowledge give, to recompense

The happy ignorance it cost? Man gave
His heaven to gain it; what was his reward?
Deep, lasting misery!

Sweet star! can those in thy bright sphere behold
Our fallen world? do they not weep to view
Our blighting sorrows? and do they not veil
Their brows in shame, to see Heaven's choicest gifts
Profaned and trampled by our maddening passions?
Surely this world is now as beautiful!
As 'twas in its earliest prime; the earth still blooms
With flowers and brilliant verdure; the dark trees
Are thick with foliage, and the mountains tower
In proud sublimity; the waters glide
All smoothly 'mid the green, enameled mead,
Or dash o'er broken cliffs, flinging their spray
In fantastic whirls.

Surely 'tis fair
As it could be before the wasting flood
Had whelmed it. Let us forth and gaze upon
The face of nature. All is peaceful now,
Yet man will tread there too; cities will rise
Where now the bird sings; thousands will dwell
Where all is loneliness; but will it be
More beautiful?

No; where the wild flowers spring,
Where nought but the bird's note is heard, we may
Find friends in every leaf; each simple bud
Speaks to the heart and fills it with the sweet,
Soft tenderness of childhood; but vain man
Makes it a peopled wilderness: the blight
Of disappointment and distrust is found

Wherever man has made his troubled home;
And the most fearful desert is the spot
Where he best loves to dwell.

O, let me hope, while gazing on thy light,
Sweet star, that yet a peaceful home is left
For those sad spirits who have found this world
All sin and sorrow. Haply in thy sphere
I yet may dwell, when cleansed from all stains
Of passions that to darkly dwell within
This throbbing heart. O! had I early died
I might have been a pure and sinless child
In some sweet planet; and my only toil,
To light my censer by the sun's bright rays,
And fling to fire forever towards the throne
Of the Eternal One.

A LITANY

When the sun of joy shines brightest,
And our steps on earth are lightest;
When to songs of quiet pleasure
Every pulse keeps joyful measure;
When no storm-cloud hovers o'er us,
And no darkness lies before us —
From the evil shapes that seem
Then from dangers lurking nigh,
All unmarked by human eye;
From the serpent in life's bowers,
Coiled beneath the fairest flowers;
From evil thoughts that hide
Even most joys abide —
Good Lord, deliver us!

When a rugged path we tread,
And the heart grows faint with dread;
When o'er waters wild and dark
Drifts our lone and helmless bark,
While the stars wax dim and pale,
Our hopes of succor fail;
When to heaven we lift our eyes,
And the waves around us rise,
Feeling that our God is there, —
O! in answer to our prayer,
Good Lord deliver us!

When the hour of death draws near,
And the soul is filled with fear;
When, with lingering step and slow,
Onward to the grave we go,
Turning from the world of light
T'ward the realms of endless night, —
Then from the demons that assail us;
When the powers of nature fail us;
Fancies of a sick man's dream,
Yet which come with fearful power,
Tempting us in life's last hour —
Good Lord, deliver us!

When the awful trump shall sound,
Startling the world's remotest bound;
When earth's charnel-house shall pour
Its myriads forth to life once more;
When, shrinking, trembling, fearful, all
Before thy glorious footstool fall, —
From the judgments that await

The spirit unregenerate;
From the sinner's guilty shame,
The gnawing worm, the quenchless flame, —
Good Lord, deliver us!

PEACE

O seek not in marble halls of pride,
Where gushing fountains fling their silver tide,
Their wealth of freshness toward the summer sky;
The echoes of a palace are too loud, —
They but give back the footsteps of the crowd,
Who throng about some idol raised on high,
Whose ermined robe and pomp of rich array,
But serve to hide the false one's feet of clay.

Nor seek her form in poverty's low vale,
Where, touched by want, the bright cheek waxes pale,
And the heart faints with sordid care opprest,
Where pining discontent has left its trace
Deep and abiding in each haggard face.
Not there, not there Peace builds her halcyon nest;
Wild revel scares her from wealth's towering dome,
And misery fights her from a lowly home.

Nor dwells she in cloister, where the sage
Ponders the mystery of the time-stained page,
Delving with feeble hand the classic mine;
The bitter yearnings for a deathless name,
That round the student's heart like serpents twine;
Ambition's fever burns within his breast;
Can Peace, sweet Peace, abide with such a guest?

Search not within the city's crowded mart,
Where the low, whispered music of the heart
Is all unheard amid the clang of gold;
O! never yet did Peace her chaplet twine
To lay upon base mammon's sordid shrine,
Where earth's most precious things are bought and sold;
Thrown on that pile, the "pearl of price" would be
Despised, because unfit for merchantry.

Go! hie thee to God's altar; kneeling there,
List to the mingled voices of fervent prayer
That swells around thee in the sacred fane,
Or catch the solemn organ's pealing note
When grateful praises on the still air float,
And the freed soul forgets earth's heavy chain;
And learn that Peace, is always found
In her eternal home on holy ground.

SONG

When the summer sunlight closes,
And each weary flower reposes,
When the evening breezes move,
Like whispers of a spirit's love, —
Then to Heaven your voices raise,
'Tis the hour of prayer and praise.

When the tempest cloud is breaking,
And the thunder's voice is waking,
When across the brow of night
Lurid lightning flashes bright, —
Then to Heaven in heart draw near,
'Tis the hour of holy fear.

Offer not your vows in sadness,
Raise the exulting song of gladness;
To the world God's works are shown,
To the world His praise be known;
Sound with the harp and timbrel free,
The glories of the Deity.

SUNSET

Farewell, farewell, thou setting sun!
I love thy gentle ray,
Thus brightening when thy task is done,
The dying day's decay;
It seems the pardoning smile of Heaven
O'er errors past and sins forgiven.

'Twas 'neath such glowing skies as this,
In fancy a high-wrought hour,
The first the living soul of song
O'erwhelmed me with its power;
Aye, from thy ray was drawn the fire
That lit my heart's funereal pyre.

O, many a change since then has past
Across this wayward heart;
Then I could almost weep to see
Thy gentle light depart;
But now I love thy fading ray,
For with it sinks another day.

Farewell, farewell, thou setting sun!
Thy last faint smile is gone;
Thou goest to make another clime
A bright and smiling dawn.

But ah! too soon thy morning beam
Will wake me from soft slumber's dream.

Farewell, farewell, thou setting sun!
I will not thus complain,
What though the dawning light will wake
My heart to thoughts of pain?
Will not wake my spirit, too?
Are there no duties left to do?

Farewell, farewell, thou setting sun!
I love thy gentle ray,
When thus calm feelings can look back
Upon a well-spent day,
And bid me seek new strength from Him
Before whose brow thy light is dim.

STANZAS

Aye, rear thine altar to Ideal Love,
And heap with costliest sacrifice the shrine;
The fairest chaplet fancy ever wove
From thought's most precious jewels, there should shine.

Aye read thine altar high, and on it lay
All that thy nature has of highest, best;
Bid thy mindcoin new wealth there day by day
And in thy lavish offering be thou blest.

But write no name upon the altar stone,
Shape out no image of thy soul's bright dreams,
Adore the unseen spirit-god alone,
Nor crown a mortal brow with heaven's own beams.

The fantasies that thrill thine every vein,
The pearls that melt in passion's burning cup,
Youth's many-colored dreams, half joy, half pain,
Its vows so true, so lightly offered up —

O mingle not the sweets of daily life
With the rich gifts of thy soul's ideal claims!
Thy human nature has its woes and strife,
Its strong requirements and its cherished aims.

The love that from an earthly fountain springs
Alone can satisfy the human quest;
The bird that highest soars, on strongest wings,
Yet stoops to earth to find a quiet nest.

But recognize thy yearnings, vague and vain,
As dim remembrances of that bright world
Whence thou wert missioned on some task of pain
Or haply for a parent's errors hurled.

Till God has loosed thy being's weary bond,
That angel light will flash o'er heart and brain,
Filling thy soul with aspirations fond
And winning thee to thy lost heaven again.

SONNET

Sorrow has changed all nature to my view,
The woods are still as green, the fields as gay;
The stars are still as bright, the sky as blue,
As when they charmed me in my childhood's day;
But now in all their beauty I can see
Something that ever 'minds me of decay, —
Some leafless branch deforms the stately tree,
Some blight still lingers on the buds of May,
The starry watchers wear a softened light
As if I gazed on them through gathering tears;
But when I turn to you pure sky, a bright
And glorious vision to my mind appears,
Making this earth seem dull beyond compare,
Since only heaven above is changeless as 'tis fair.

HOLY CHRONICLES

CHRIST IN THE TEMPEST

Midnight was on the mighty deep,
And darkness filled the boundless sky,
While 'mid the raging wind was heard
The sea bird's mournful cry;
For tempest clouds were mustering wrath
Across the seaman's trackless path.

It came at length; one fearful gust
Rent from the mast the shivering sail,
And drove the hapless bark along,
The plaything of the gale;
While fearfully the lightning's glare
Fell on the pale brows gathered there.

But the was One o'er whose bright face
Unmarked the vivid lightnings flashed;
And on whose stirless, prostrate form
Unfelt the sea-spray dashed;
For 'mid the tempest fierce and wild,
He slumbered like a wearied child.

O! who could look upon that face,
And feel the sting of coward fear?
Though hell's fierce demons raged around,
Yet Heaven itself was here;
For who that glorious brow could see
Nor own a present Deity?

With hurried fear they press around
The lowly Saviour's humble bed,
As if his very touch had power
To shield their souls from dread;
While, cradled on the raging deep,
He lay in calm and tranquil sleep.

Vainly they struggled with their fears,
But wilder still the tempest woke,
Till from their full and o'erfraught hearts
The voice of terror broke:
"Behold! we sink beneath the wave;
We perish, Lord! but thou canst save."

Slowly he rose; and mild rebuke
Shone in his soft and heavenly-lit eye;
"O ye of little faith," he cried,
"Is not your master nigh?
Is not your hope of succor just?
Why know ye not in whom to put ye trust?"

He turned away, and conscious power
Dilated his majestic form,
And o'er the boiling sea he bent,
The ruler of the storm;
Earth to its centre felt the thrill,
As low he murmured: Peace! Be Still!

Hark to the burst of meeting waves,
The roaring of the angry sea!
A moment more, and all is hushed
In deep tranquility;
While not a breeze is near to break
The mirrored surface of the lake.

Then on the stricken hearts of all,
Fell anxious doubt and holy awe,
As timidly the gazed on him
Whose will was nature's law
"What man is this," they cry, "whose word
E'en by the raging sea is heard?"

THE HYMN IN THE TEMPEST

Strange forms and stranger minds and hearts were met
In the frail bark which bore a precious freight
To the new land of promise. Men had left
The scenes of childhood and the marts of wealth
To seek a home in the dim forest's shades,
Where, all unchecked by man's misguided power,
Their prayers might rise unfettered to their God.
'Twas one of those bright days when nature seems
To hold quiet sabbath, when the earth
And sea are hushed in silence. The dark waves
Scarce laved the sides of the tall ship, and played
Around the keel in sportiveness. There stood
Within the humble cabin a small band
Of Hernhuth's lowly children; and thus rose
Their hymn of thanksgiving: —

Ancient of Days!
With meek and lowly hearts we come
To pour the exciting hymn of praise
To thee, who ledst us from the home
Where our feet were wont to roam,
O'er the wild untrodden deep
Where the scaly monsters sleep.

Thy mighty will
Thy children in their peril saves,
The rushing winds are hushed and still,
And slumber bound the tumbling waves
Whose deep abyss yawn like graves.
Tidings of the Heavenly King,
Wonders of thy power and grace,
Saviour of the fallen race!

Glory to God!
For within the trackless wild
Where foot of man has never trod,
Where never heaven-sent peace has smiled
On scenes by pagan rites defiled,
Soon our hymns with grateful note
On the fragrant breeze shall float,
And upon the air shall swell
The sweetest sound — the sabbath bell.

Hark! a loud crash,
A sudden wrenching of lofty masts,
A burst of mighty winds and mountain waves.
On came the sea: gathering new strength it came,
Till on the reeling vessel full it broke,

Rending its very seams. Between the decks
It rushed in fury, pouring its full tide,
Sweeping all things before it; then arose
The shriek of a woman's terror, and the groan
That told man's sterner agony.

Unmoved
The meek Hernhuthers stood: woman was there
With her calm placid brow; and childhood, too,
With sunny smiles yet lurking on its lip,
Though softened to that pleasant gravity
Which speaks the reverence of an untrained heart, —
A vague and indistinct, but holy fear:
Yet not an eyelid trembled, not a cheek
Blanched at the sight of terror; mother's prest
The infants to their bosoms, as the wave
Curled foaming round their feet; and sires, too, raised
Their bright-haired boys above the briny stream;
But not a murmur rose. The hymn went on;
A moment it had passed, then rose again
The low, sweet voice, the deep, full tone — but changed
The spirit of the hymn: —

Maker of heaven and earth!
In peril's fearful hour we call on thee;
From thee the mighty elements have birth,
Thou mad'st, and can still the raging sea.

Father, which art in heaven!
We are thy children, fashioned by thy hand, —
The fleeting breath of life by thee was given, —
As suppliants now before thy face we stand.

Son of the Father God!
Thou who didst walk unharmed upon the wave,
Thou who, for us, did kiss the avenging rod,
Hear now thy children's prayer, O! hear and save!
Redeemer of the world!
If thou hast doomed us to this bitter death,
If in the boiling strife of waters hurled,
We must resign to thee our struggling breath —

Grant us thy holy power
To turn unmoved from all that binds the heart,
To give ourselves to thee in peril's hour,
And as in faith we live, in faith depart!

The tempest cloud had passed; the sudden burst
Of elemental fury gone by;
And the waves leaped against the vessel's side
With low moaning, like the murmured sounds
That mar the quiet slumbers of child
Wearied with its waywardness.

The hour
Of peril was forgotten; but one heart
Was troubled with its many doubts and fears,
And to the humble pastor of the flock
That looked so fearless in the face of death,
He came with anxious air: "Had you no fear
That thus your song was poured upon the winds,
When its wild rush was like the knell of death?"
"God rides the tempest; wherefore should we fear?"
Was the meek answer. — "But your wives, your babes,
Have they no terrors?" — "Surely not: they know
That God their Father rules the winds and waves;
They know that death but point the way to Him;
And who would shrink to meet a parent's face?"

CHARLES RUSSELL

THE POOL OF BETHESDA

Tranquil Bethesda's waters lay,
No breeze the surface stirred,
When sudden through the brightening air
A rustling wing was heard;
Then loudly rose the joyous cry:
The angel of the pool is nigh!"

Well might they shout, the lame, the blind,
The fevered who had lain
Beside Bethesda's healing wave,
Through many a day of pain;
They knew it was the destined hour
When God would show his pitying power.

Then with the selfishness that marks
Deep misery, they rushed
Toward the holy fount that now
With heaven sent freshness gushed;
For he who first should reach its brink
New being from its wave might drink.

But there was one who stirless lay
Upon his weary couch;
Nor sought amid the hurrying crowd
The troubled waters to touch;
But in his bitter sigh was heard
The agony of "hope deferred."

Almost reproachfully he turned
His eye upon the stream;
When, lo! a gentle voice awoke,
Like music in a dream,
So soft, so sweet its accents stole, —
"My brother! wilt thou not be whole?"

Slowly he turned his feeble frame,
And gazed upon a face
Of more than a woman's loveliness,
Of more than kingly grace;
"Alas! in vain my will," he cried,
"I cannot reach Bethesda's tide.

"In more than infant feebleness,
Through long and changeless years,
I've lain beside this healing pool
And yet no help appears;
For ere my palsied limbs draw nigh,
The hour of mercy is gone by."

The Saviour bent his noble form,
A heavenly smile passed o'er
His placid lip: "Arise!" he cried,
"Go hence and sin no more!"
Lo touched by those almighty hands,
Once more in manhood's strength he stands.

Surely this deed of wondrous power
A truth to *us* imparts;
When Heaven's best gifts have not the skill
To heal our broken hearts,
May we not look through faith to thee
The first-born of eternity?

THE MORAVIAN BURIAL GROUND

'Twas one of those sweet days when spring wakes
Her gentlest zephyrs and her softest light,
Wooing the wild flowers in the sunny brakes,
And winning the young bird to joyous flight;
While rose the lulling murmur of the bee
'Mid the sweet sound of Nature's jubilee.

Our loitering feet unconsciously we turned
Toward a green and solitary lane;
A pure, calm spirit in our bosom burned,
And feelings saddened, though unmixed with pain:
O! surely then we were in a fitting mood
To ponder on the grave's dread solitude.

Through a low gate our quiet steps we bent;
Was this sweet, lonely spot a burial place?
Here was no urn, no sculptured monument,
But o'er spring had shed her loveliest trace;
For the bright verdure of the fragrant bloom
Of the wild violet, decked each smiling tomb.

A lowly mound of earth, an humble stone,
Traced with the name of him who lay beneath,
A name still dear to love, though never known
To fame, were all that spoke of dreaded death;
Fresh grass, and flowers, and scented herbs were there,
Filling with brightness earth, with odors air.

High swelled my heart as 'mid those graves I trod;
I felt life's nothingness in that calm hour;
My spirit knew the presence of its God,
And bowed submissive to Almighty power;
While humbly now I deemed I ne'er should shrink
To drain the cup that earthly love must drink.

I had been an idolator — aye, still
My heart was vowed upon an earthly shrine;
Though checked a moment by that holy thrill,
I knew my bosom never could resign
Its deep idolatry till life was past;
Had I not cause to fear Heaven's frown at last?

For there, with eyelids closed in changeless night,
The mother and her sinless child lay;
In the same hour death breathed o'er both his blight,
And in one pang their spirits passed away:
The all of mother's feelings she had known
Were the keen throe, the agony alone.

Alas for earthly joy, and hope, and love,
Thus stricken down e'en in their holiest hour!
What deep, heart-wringing anguish they must prove
Who live to weep the blasted tree and flower!
O, woe, deep woe, the earthly love's fond trust,
When all it once has worshipped lies in dust!

There was one hillock decked beyond the rest,
Where rue, and thyme, and violets were sighing;
No trace of earth defaced its verdant breast;
The wild bee o'er the sunny flowers was flying.
Or hiding, 'mid the odorous buds and leaves,
Beneath the dewy veil the evening weaves.

There slept the patriarch of fourscore years,
Whose long life like an April day had closed
In smiles and sunshine after clouds and tears;
Now calm in death his ancient form reposed;
With oft affection's pearly tears bedewed
The flowers that decked his peaceful solitude.

Lo! while we gazed with slow and noiseless tread
A female form drew nigh; her right hand bore
A water urn; and o'er the unconscious dead
Low she bent, its freshening dews to pour,
Till the flowers 'neath the sun gleamed up,
Each bearing a rich gem within its cup.

Ten years have past since he who slumbered there
Had cast aside the weight of clay, and yet
His grave still fondly claimed a daughter's care;
Still was it visited with deep regret:
Such was the love of hearts o'er which no trace
Of earth had passed affection to efface.

Then with tumultuous feelings all subdued
By death's undreaded presence, I awoke
My song's low murmurs in that solitude,
And thus my half-breathed whispers softly broke: —

When in the shadow of the tomb,
This heart shall rest,
O, lay me where the spring-flowerets bloom
On earth's green breast.

But ne'er in vaulted chambers lay
My lifeless form;
Seek not of such poor, worthless prey
To cheat the worm.

In some sweet city of the dead
I fain would sleep,
Where flowers may deck my narrow bed,
And night dews weep.

And raise not the sepulchral urn
To mark the spot:
Enough if by love alone
'Tis ne'er forgot.

BYRON IN CERTOSA CEMETERY

"IMPLORA PACE!" 'tis the cry
Of some meek child of want and care
Whose life has been a long, long sigh,
A weary struggle with despair.
"Implora Pace!" 'tis the prayer
Low breathed from out a contrite heart,
When, turning from things that are,
Through death's dark shadows to depart.

"Implora Pace!" hark! the groan
Bursts from the quivering lip of one
Who proudly stands on earth alone,
'Mid many stars the only sun.
He bends above the lonely tomb;
Dark thoughts have dimmed his flashing eye,
His brow wears sorrow's heaviest gloom;
Then list his agonizing cry —

'Implora Pace!' I have quaffed
From pleasures wine-cup mantling high,

Was found the peace for which I sigh.
In love, earth's best deceit, I sought
The rest for which my bosom pined;
With bliss, deep bliss, the dream was fraught,
Its madness still remains behind.

'Implora Pace!' I have run
With speed unslackened glory's race
In the world's wondering sight have won
Its bays my boyish brow to grace;
My name is heard from every tongue,
My words on every heart imprest,
My strains in every clime are sung,
Yet fame brings not my spirit rest.

'Implora Pace!' I have tried
All the earth knows of joy or pain
Its bliss, its woes, its hope, its pride,
All, all alike, are worse than vain,
Withered and old in heart I stand
Upon the brink of death's dark wave,
And hope, aye hope no better land
Awaits the soul beyond the grave.

'Implora Pace!' all I seek
Is rest — the soul's eternal rest.
Thou mouldering clay beneath me, speak!
Say, will death satisfy my quest?
Thou canst not tell — I dare not think —
Child-like at phantom forms I quake;
Yet fain of death's dark stream would drink,
My feverish spirit's thirst to slake.

HEARTACHE

A LAMENT

"O'er the wide waters of the swelling sea,
Whose mystic music once I loved to hear,
But whose low moaning now must ever be,
The voice of death and sorrow to mine ear,
Echoed by many a wild and restless wave,
I pour my wail above a brother's grave.

Not in the lap of gentle mother earth,
Whose worn and wearied children come to lay
Their aching heads on her who gave them birth,
Glad to forget life's long and toilsome day —
Not on her quiet bosom didst thou close
Thine eyes, my brother, in their last repose.

Thine was a death of agony — a brief
And mortal struggle with the foaming deep;
Yes, while we mourn with unavailing grief,
Thou, pillowed on the shifting surge, dost sleep
As tranquilly as if spring's earliest bloom
Was showered in roses on thy early tomb.

THE MOTHER'S SOLACE

I knew thou wert mortal! aye, my heart
Thrilled with vague terror, even while the beams
Of they soft, loving eyes could still impart
A joy as sinless as thine own pure dreams;
Thou wert too like a thing of heavenly birth
To tarry long upon this darkened earth.

I knew thou wert mortal; the blue vein
Whose delicate tracery adorned thy brow,
I knew might bear the rushing tide of pain,
Instead of life's pure current, in its flow,
I knew disease thy cheek might pale,
And the hour come when flesh and heart should fail.

I knew thou wert mortal; yet my tears
Have flowed in rivers o'er thy lowly bed;
The joys of life, the hopes of coming years,
Were crushed when thou were numbered with the dead,
And life itself must cease ere I forget
The bitter yearnings of my vain regret.

I knew thou wert mortal; but the God
Who filled with deathless love a mother's heart,
Meant not that she should kiss the chastening rod
Without feeling of its its anguished smart.
Can it be sin to bow the mourning head
When even Jesus wept o'er Lazarus dead?

I knew thou wert mortal; but can naught
Bring solace to the soul in sorrow's hour?
Is there not consolations in the thought
That Christ has robbed the grave of half its power?
Not without hope, beloved one, do I weep,
Thou yet shall waken from thy dreamless sleep.

I knew thou wert mortal; but the bright
And glorious beauty of thine earthly face
Would seem all dim beside the radiant light
Which crowns thy spirit now with cherub grace;
I know thee now immortal, – and I trust
To meet thee again, though dust return to dust.

STANZAS ON THE DEATH OF A SISTER

Weep for the dead! 'tis meet that tears should consecrate the spot
Where sleep the loves of better years, the hopes that cheered our lot;
When the once peopled heart is left all desolate and lone,
'Tis meet that tears should gem the trace of each departed one;
Yet not in hopeless grief we mourn, — we know that they are blest,
"Where the wicked cease from troubling, and the weary are at rest."

Weep for the dead! A vacant place is left beside our hearth,
We miss a low and gentle voice with its tones of quiet mirth;
The meek and placid face that seemed a moonlight ray to shed,
Now, veiled forever from our view, rests with the dreamless dead;
Yet not in hopeless grief we mourn — that spotless soul is blest;
"Where the wicked cease from troubling, and the weary are at rest."

Weep for the dead! As summer showers refresh the thirsting earth,
So on the scathed heart fall the tears that mourn departed worth;
As summer's fairest flowers are nursed by April's weeping skies.
Surely the dead may claim our tears, e'en though we know them blest,
"Where the wicked cease from troubling, and the weary are at rest.

Weep for the dead! The bounteous God who gave us hearts to feel,
Meant not that we their hidden founts of tenderness should steal;
How could we learn our mighty debt of gratitude to pay
For blessings left, if nought we recked of blessings snatched away?
Yes! We may weep for the sainted dead, e'en though we know them blest,
"Where the wicked cease troubling, and the weary are at rest."

ELEGAIC STANZAS

Thou has left us, and forever!
The light of those sweet eyes
Will beam upon us never,
Till we meet above the skies.
Life's sunshine was around thee,
The world looked glad and bright,
And the ties of love that bound thee
Might have stayed thy spirit's flight;
But the bonds that earth entwineth
Are all too weak to stay,
When far off Heaven shineth,
The spirit's upward way.

Thou hast left us, and forever!
Thy smile of quiet mirth,
Thy low sweet voice shall never
Soothe our aching hearts on earth.
The joys thy presence cherished,
Like morning dreams have fled,
And many a fair hope perished
Upon thy narrow bed.
For the love we have borne thee
Thy loss we needs must weep,
Yet, even while we mourn thee,
We envy thee thy sleep.

THE MOURNER'S APPEAL

Flowers, happy flowers methinks your tender eyes
Look kindly on me in my distress;
Dwells there no healing virtue in your sighs?
Have ye no balm the weary heart to bless?
Can ye not give from your glowing hearts
A freshness like the joy of childhood's hours?
Or must I feel, as youth departs,
Life's dial only once it wreathed in flower?

Stars, holy stars! pure watchers of the night!
Is there no beam that points the way to hope?
Amid a world of so much gladsome light,
Must I ever in thick darkness grope?
O chase this wild horror from my thought;
Let me but feel Heaven pities my deep woe;
My future years are with such anguish fraught,
I look upward, — peace dwells not below.

Since first my soul took cognizance of life,
I've looked on Nature with a lover's eye;
Amid the world's bitter toil and strife,
I still have felt her gentle influence nigh:
Yet now when in agony I come,
Fleeing to her in refuge from despair,
Her shrine is cold, her oracles are dumb,
No sympathy nor solace wait me there.

'Tis that mine eyes are dimmed with frequent tears,
Else would I see balm in every flower,
And find a light to chase my gloomy fears
In every star that gems the evening hour;
'Tis that my soul is dark with sinful doubt,
And finds no promise in the world so fair,
Ere would each star and fragrant bud give out
Its pledge that God, our Hope, is everywhere.

EPITAPHS ON A YOUNG LADY

I.

Called from life's banquet ere one rose grew pale
Which love had wreathed around thy youthful brow,
Death summoned thee to joys that never fail,
And made thee thus the angel thou art now.

II.

Gifted with all that life could bless,
Thine early death we must deplore;
For earth hath now one saint less,
Though heaven hath gained one angel more.

STANZAS

Mournfully my spirit turns
To dreams of olden time,
And oft my heart within me burns
When I hear some old world rhyme;

And ever has poesy been to me
The Atlantis of Time's wide sea;
I have steered full often my weary bark
For that green isle in the waters dark;
But never my foot might press its shore,
And I turn to actual life once more
Mournfully, O, mournfully!

Mournfully doth my bosom pine
For the fantasies of youth;
And I would that fancy now could shine
With a light like that of truth;
I would lift my worldly laden thought
To the realms with so much beauty fraught,
I would catch again the glorious gleam
That filled my soul with heavenly beam
Ere my earthly hopes and earthly fears
Brought my feelings back to this vale of tears,
Mournfully, O, mournfully!

Mournfully do my tear-drops fall
On the poet's pictured page,
And fain would I the dreams recall
That gladdened life's golden age;
But I bartered those treasures long ago,
For happiness such as few can know,
Nor would I recall the feverish past,
With its wild unrest and its pang at last;
Yet the voice of song hath magic still,
And its gentle tones can my spirit thrill,
Mournfully, O, mournfully!

FRAGMENT

Whence come this heaviness of soul,
These dark presentiments of coming ill,
The dreams that spurn at reason's sage control,
And these thick-gathering fantasies, and chill
The heart with sudden terror? Are they sent
As portents of the future to fulfill
The dark decrees of fate? or only meant
To snap the strength of mind, man's noblest battlement?

We know not whence they come, nor can we tell
Whether they flee; we only feel their power
Withering our hearts be some mysterious spell,
And stealing o'er us even in the hour
When hope and joy are brightest, till we cower
Before those shadows, as the warrior steed
Undaunted braves the battle's iron shower,
And yet will quiver like the shaken reed,
If through a moonlit wood his onward pathway lead.

O, man! how strange a mystery thou art,
The noblest yet the weakest of creation;
Unable to subdue thine own proud heart,
Yet swaying oft the fortunes of a nation.
God-like in thy high attributes and station,
Worm-like in each groveling desire,
Yet even in they lowliest degradation,
Showing forth glimpses of that heavenly fire
Which, though earth-stained and dim, can never quite expire.

Ye who in the field of human life
Quickening seeds of wisdom fain would sow,
Pause not for the angry tempest's strife,
Shrink not from noontide's fervid glow;

Labor on, while yet the light of day
Shed abroad its pure and blessèd ray.
For night cometh!

Ye who at man's mightiest engine stand,
Molding noble thought into opinion,
O stay not for weariness your hand.
Till ye fix the bounds of truth's dominion;
Labor on, while yet the light of day
Sheds upon your toil its blessèd ray,
For night cometh!

Ye to whom the prophet-voice is given,
Stirring men as by a trumpet call,
Utter forth the oracles of Heaven, —
Earth gives back the echoes as they fall;
O speak out, while yet the light of day
Breaks life's slumber with its blessèd ray,
For night cometh!

Ye who in home's narrow circle dwell,
Feeding Love's flame upon the household hearth,
Weave the silken bond, and wake the spell
Binding heart to heart throughout the earth;
Gentle toil is yours; the light of day
On nought sheds its blessèd ray,
For night cometh!

Diverse though our paths in life may be,
Each is sent a mission to fulfill;
Fellow workers in the world are we,
While we seek to do our Master's will;
But our doom is to labor while the day
Light us on our task with blessèd ray,
For night cometh!

Fellow workers are we; hour by hour
Human tools are shaping Heaven's great schemes,
Till we see no limit to man's power,
And reality outstrips old dreams;
Toil and trouble therefore weep:
In God's acre ye shall calmly sleep
When night cometh!

STANZAS

I have no heart! I know not where
The wild and restless thing has fled;
It lives not in a mortal breast,
Nor is it with the dead.

I have no heart! love, hope, and joy;
Stir not the current of my life,
Nor know I aught of rapture's thrill,
Nor passion's fearful strife.

I have no heart! too early chilled
It slumbered ne'er to wake again,
E'en as the frozen traveler sleeps
Through all life's parting pain.

I have no heart! no power can wake
My spirit from it's heavy trance;
Alike to me are love's sweet looks,
Or hatred's withering glance.

I have no heart! nor would I call
The restless thing to life once more,
E'en if a wish could give me all
I sought in days of yore.

STANZAS

Dearest, a mournful strain is all the New Year's gift I bring,
For images of bygone years throng round me as I sing;
My spirit's joyousness is gone, I can no longer fling
The sunshine of a happy heart o'er every earthly thing.

A shadow lies upon my path which naught can chase away;
Save the great Sun of Righteousness with healing in its ray;
A shadow from the mountain dark o'er which our feet must tread,
To meet again our loved of yore, our treasures of the dead.

That shadow lies upon my path, and pleasures 'neath its gloom,
Like flowerets grown in darkness, now have lost their brilliant bloom;
My days of buoyant happiness have with my youth been spent,
Yet will I still strive what e'er my lot, therewith to be content!

Alas! the magic cup of life but sparkles near the brim;
The music of this weary world is but a morning hymn;
And like the dream of night of our youthful days depart,
Leaving but half-traced images within the saddened heart.

Yes, all the joys in after years are like Egyptian feasts,
Where Memory's shrouded form sits first amid the guests;
In vain the gay laugh circles round, the wine cup mantles high,
The glitter of unshed tears lights up the listless eye.

INQUIETUDE

Methought the icy hand of Time had chilled
The gushing fount of passion in my breast;
Methought that reason's power, for aye, had stilled
The bitter struggles of my heart's unrest.

Cold, calm, and self-possessing, I had deemed
In quiet now to view life slip away,
Forgetting much that once my soul had dreamed,
And lengthening out in peace my little day.

Safe in indifference, I had vainly hoped
To scorn the sympathy I might not share,
And little thought mine own hand would have oped
My bosom's portal to returning care.

How burns the blush of shame upon my cheek,
How bend to earth in grief my haughty brow,
When thus I find myself disarmed and weak
Before the ideal shapes that haunt me now!

O God! how long, misled by erring thought,
Shall I grope darkly in feeling's maze?
When shall I be by Time's sad lessons taught,
And reach my home of rest in quiet ways?

FRAGMENT

The fire within my soul burns dim and low,
Like some neglected cresset's dying glow,
And my heart beats fitfully and slow,
E'en as a bell in ruined turret hung,
When by the gusty night breeze feebly swung,
Making no pleasant sounds, as to and fro
Through the thick air its dull vibrations go.

The light is darkened on my spirit's shrine,
And silent are the oracles of thought;
Hushed are the echoes of that voice divine
Whose faintest tone my inner sense once caught;

No bright descending angel flings
From off his glorious wings
The hues of Paradise o'er earthly things;
No heavenly dreams like seraphs round me throng,
Filling life's temple with the voice of song.

Fain would I lift
My soul in adoration, but no more
Upon my lips I feel the precious gift
Of eloquent utterance, as in days of yore;
Yet there are times when o'er my dull brain floats
A strain of fleeting music, and the notes
Seem like articulate words; then would I fain
Forget the weary weight of wasting pain,
And pour forth all the love that now lies mute,
Like tones hidden in a stringless lute.

SONNET

A bruised and broken heart , O God! I bring
To lay upon thine altar; It has striven
Rebellious 'gainst thy will, and madly given
Its precious things to idols and doth cling
E'en yet to earthly love, whose venomed sting
Has poisoned all the charities of life,
Turning its life-blood into tears and strife.
O let me nestle 'neath Dove's pure wing!
Send down the Comforter, that He may lay
The balm of healing on my aching brow,
And with his radiant presence chase away
The dark and frowning shapes that haunt me now,
For I am fainting 'neath my great despair,

Crushed by the burden of a granted prayer.

SOMETHING BEYOND

Heart! weary heart! what mean thy wild unrest?
Hast thou not tasted of life's every pleasure?
With all that mortals seek, thy lot is blest,
Yet dost thou ever chant in solemn measure,
"Something Beyond!"

Heart! weary heart! canst thou not find repose
In the sweet calm of friendship's pure devotion?
Amid the peace which sympathy bestows,
Still dost thou murmur with repressed emotion,
"Something beyond!"

Heart! weary heart! too idly hast thou poured
Thy music and thy perfume in the blast;
Now beggared in affection's treasure hoard,
Thy cry is still, —thy saddest and thy last, —
"Something beyond!"

Heart! weary heart! O cease thy wild unrest;
Earth cannot satisfy thy bitter yearning;
But onward, upward speed thy lonely quest,
And hope to find, where Heaven's pure stars are burning,
"Something beyond!"

COURAGE

SONNET

Self-missioned leader through Creation's maze!
Dost though interpret thus God's mighty scheme
Weaving the cobweb fantasies of a dream
O'er each gray vestige of His mystic ways?
When thus midst chaos thou did blindly grope,
Gathering new links for matter's heavy chain,
Dwelt there not in the soul the secret hope
That some strong truth would rend the bond of pain
Which fixed thee to Progression's iron wheel?
O teach not suffering earth such a hopeless creed —
Too heavy were her curse if doomed to feel
That in her frequent hour of bitter need,
Her lifted eye of prayer could only see
Necessity's stern laws graven on eternity.

SONNET

Alas! for those who quench the holy spark
Of inspiration in their secret soul,
Yielding their natures up to earth's control,
Until the mental sight grows dark,
And thought no longer seeks a lofty mark,

While the heart drains life's enervating bowl,
And freights with all its hope some helmless bark!
Alas! Alas! On earthly shrines we lay
The incense we should offer up to Heaven,
We lavish on an idol of today
That love for infinitude was given,
Till from our souls the light fades slow away,
And clouds of doubt and fear are o'er our spirits driven.

SABBATH MORNING

There is a quiet beauty in the sky
A balmy freshness in the tranquil air,
That fills my mind with holiest thoughts, my heart
With gentlest feelings; e'en the glorious sun
With softer splendor seems to usher in
The peaceful Sabbath. Well may it be called
A day of rest, when it thus sweetly stills
Not merely the city's busy hum,
But the fierce warfare of the human heart.

O, how could passion wake in this calm hour?
E'en my proud soul is humbled, and I lift
Mine eyes to Heaven, not now in wild reproof.
Murmuring at its decrees, but with deep
And calm submission of wounded spirit,
Praying for strength to suffer. Well I know
My lot is sorrow; pain, and sickness, aye,
The sickness of hearth and early death,
These fill the measure of my destiny.

And O, how often do my feelings rise
In vain rebellion, when with weary limb
I press the couch of sickness! or when pain,
The worst of pain, wrings my lone heart, how oft
Does my worn spirit that soon may come
The rest too long delayed! but when I feel
The fragrant breath of heaven, e'en though as now
It fans a feverish brow, or stirs across
A cheek that tears have faded, it awakes
My slumbering energies. The Power that stills
The raging of the swelling seas, can stay
The wild tempestuous waves of earthly feeling,
And teach me calm endurance.

CONFIDENCE IN HEAVEN

It was in vain the weary spirit strives
With that which doth consume it: there is born
A strength from suffering which can laugh to scorn
The stroke of sorrow, even though it rives
Our very heart-strings; but the grief that lives
Forever in the heart, and day by day
Wastes the soul's high wrought energies away,
And wears the lofty spirit down, and gives
Its own dark hue to life, O! who can bear?
Yet, as the black and threatening tempest bring
New fragrance to earth's flowers and tints more fair
So beneath sorrow's nurture virtues spring.
Youth, health, and hope may fade, but there is left
A soul that trusts in Heaven, though thus bereft.

DEVOTION

Mine eyes are pained with watching, for the brow
Of heaven has lost its crown of starry light,
And soon upon my dim and dazzled sight
The gladdening morn will come with all its glow
Of new-born loveliness; then let me bow
The knee to Heaven, and lift my heart in prayer,
Ere earth with all its vain and troublous care
Comes back upon my spirit, ere the flow
Of holy thought be stayed: yet 'tis for thee
That I would pray, beloved one, for thy lot
I dare to question God's untold decree,
And ask the bliss my own heart knoweth not;
Be thy path marked with light! enough for me
If in thy glory's hour I be not quite forgot.

HOW WILL YE THINK OF ME

When life's false oracles, no more replying
To baffled Hope, shall mock my weary quest;
When in the grave's cold shadow calmly lying,
This heart at last has found its earthly rest —
How will ye think of me? O gentle friends,
How will ye think of me?

Perhaps the wayside flowers around ye springing,
Wasting unmarked their fragrance and their bloom,

Or some fresh fount in the forest singing
Unheard, unheeded, may recall my doom:
Will ye thus think of me?

Or let the day-beam glancing o'er the ocean
Picture my restless heart, which, like yon wave,
Reflected doubly, in wild commotion,
Each ray of light that pleasure's sunlight gave:
Will ye thus think of me?

Will ye bring back my memory's art, the gladness
That sent my fancies forth like summer birds?
Or will ye list the undertone of sadness,
Which music seldom shaped itself in words?
Will ye think thus of me?

Remember not how dreams, around me thronging,
Enticed me ever from life's lonely way,
But O! still hearken to the deep soul-longing
Whose mournful tones pervade the poet's lay, —
Will you thus think of me?

And then, forgetting every wayward feeling,
Bethink ye only that I loved ye well,
Till o'er your souls that "late remorse" is stealing
Whose voiceless anguish only tears can tell:
Will ye thus think of me? O gentle friends!
Will ye thus think of me?

"DUM SPIRO, SPERO"

"Dum spiro, spero;" while I breathe, I hope;
O! God be thanked above all else for this, —
The only gift within the world's wide scope
Which in its ceaseless promise bringeth bliss.

"Dum spiro, spero;" life and hope entwined:
Grief may o'ershadow us and pain destroy,
But in our inmost spirit is enshrined
The sweet expectancy of coming joy.

"Dum spiro, spero;" till our latest breath
Our human nature has its cherished dream;
But immortality is born of Death,
And bliss eternal dims Hope's earthly beam.